Do Something!

"I Can...I Will—*I Won't Quit!*"

Special Volume Discounts:
This book is available at special discounts when purchased in quantity for attendees, teachers and/or a fundraiser. Make one of Jim's live events everlasting by investing in an autographed copy for each teacher or attendee. For details and special pricing, please contact:

JimBballJones@gmail.com.

Cover and Interior Design by Jean Boles
https://www.upwork.com/fl/jeanboles4

Edited by Daphne Parsekian

Paperback ISBN: 978-1-7350356-0-4
E-book ISBN: 978-1-17350356-1-1

First Printed: May 2020

Do Something!

"I can...I will—*I won't quit!*"

James Jones

Dedication

I could not have written this book without the loving support of my wife, Brenda. She truly pushed me to get this project done and get it out there to help other people. Thank you, honey, for all of your support, your encouragement, and believing in me.

I also want to thank my mom for being there every step of the way throughout my journey. She was the one constant in my life growing up that I could count on. She did everything she could to support me financially, emotionally, and academically. Thanks, Mom.

I also want to thank all of the special tutors and teachers who helped me through my journey. Ms. Judy Bamer (Day) was my first tutor, and she set the stage for me to work hard and keep trying to improve. I also want to mention Mrs. Braudhurst and Mrs. Lara for all their dedication as they helped me navigate through middle school. Also in middle school, I was lucky to have one of those unique teachers who pushed me, challenged me, and encouraged me. I truly enjoyed Mrs. Dematte's English class, even though this was my hardest subject and my major weakness. Her humor and demeanor in class were awesome, and she definitely brought out the best in me. I also want to give a huge thanks to Mrs. Schuster. She taught a class called Reading in the Real World, and she made a huge impact on my reading and study skills in just the nick of time. I was a senior, and I needed someone to push me to the next level; Mrs. Schuster did that, and I owe her a debt of gratitude. Finally, I want to thank one last teacher. He wasn't one of my tutors or an English teacher who helped me with my weaknesses but a math teacher who stretched me in an area of my strength. I still use some of his sayings in my assemblies to this day. Thank you, Mr. Briggs, for making math fun and challenging. I truly enjoyed your humor, your presence, and how you taught.

Contents

Introduction

"There are no constraints on the human mind, no walls around the human spirit, no barriers to our progress except those we ourselves erect."

– Ronald Reagan

We will all face some form of adversity in our lifetime. It's naive to think otherwise. As we strive for our goals, we will all face challenges. Some of us will be born into adversity, but all of us will *face* adversity eventually. These challenges will create feelings of self-doubt, worry, and apathy. So how do we accomplish our goals and dreams when we face challenges?

Remember, how we decide to deal with our adversity will determine our level of success. Success and happiness are not out of your reach, regardless of the challenges you face.

We all experience self-doubt and insecurities. We all have shortcomings and weaknesses, but we have to make a choice: Are we are going to let them hold us back, or are we going to "Do Something" to reach our goal? As LeBron James would say, "Strive for greatness." I feel we all should be striving to become our best and constantly trying to improve and grow.

Read my story. It is mine—just as you are writing your own. You will see that I understand what it means to have adversity staring at you while you are standing at the fork in the road, trying to decide what to do next and which road to take. Take a walk with me, take a risk, and learn through my experiences how to overcome the adversity and challenges that may be in your life.

In this book, I will detail my academic life growing up in Special Education and being labeled LD ("learning disabled"). I will reflect on the lessons I learned to break through those limiting impressions or beliefs plus include strategies and ideas that I have learned from books, coaches, friends, and family on how to overcome adversity and find success. Take a walk with me, my friend.

I hope this is an inspiration and a guide to help you with adversity and will allow you to become the person you want to become. Here's to you and to finding your success and your happiness.

Chapter 1- Growing up in Special Education

"The struggle you're in today is developing the strength you need for tomorrow. Don't give up!"

- Robert Tew

Before I share my story, I would like to say that I wouldn't want to change the challenges I experienced in my life. I am who I am today because of what I had to go through growing up. Those challenges have created a stronger mindset and a stronger will to get through adversity. They have also allowed me to find my strengths and use them to improve my weaknesses. Finally, they instilled a belief in me that everyone can learn and improve over time, no matter how slow the process is.

This realization has inspired me to talk to schools as Jim "Basketball" Jones. I have had the chance to speak to students at over 8,000 schools, and my drive to reach out to students and teachers continues. We all can learn. We all can improve, and sometimes the challenges we face in life are the ones we need to help us become the person we were meant to become. Every day I have a chance to make a difference in the life of a child or a teacher through my speaking career, to help them see the possibilities and give them hope. My challenges have created my passion, which has turned into my lifelong journey of making a difference. No, I wouldn't change what I went through to have an easier life growing up, because I wouldn't be as strong nor would I be able to help so many other people. My story makes me who I am.

My story starts the summer before second grade. I was seven years old. Academically, adversity was staring me straight in the face. I was going to have to learn how to overcome dyslexia and the inability to read. This was going to take time, practice, and an attitude and mindset to not let the challenge that faced me define who I was but rather how I was going to face this challenge. I had to learn how to fight the fight.

If you know anything about dyslexia, you know it is a language-based learning disability. It involves struggling with the processing of sounds and letters into written and spoken words. Sounds can be omitted or not heard at all. The alphabet becomes a sea of symbols that have no meaning. I was not a typical first grader learning the alphabet with its sounds and letters or blending sounds together to make words. I couldn't differentiate certain sounds or letters. I couldn't hear some of them. To say I struggled is an understatement.

Jim's First Evaluation

I realized early in life that I would have to work hard just to make it to a regular classroom. As I struggled with dyslexia, I spent my first five years of school in a special education classroom. I worked with Ms. Bamer as my LD teacher and also had a speech therapist. After my first-grade year, I had a tutor, Nancy Nelson, over the summer to determine my weaknesses and my readiness for second grade. Below is a summary of the tests Nancy administered me and what she had written to my mom.

(Matching Alphabet test): He did well in alphabet matching but confused the letters b and d. This test was to see if he could match capital letters and lowercase letters by sight only. It did not deal with the sounds or the names of the letters.

(Alphabet review test): As you know, when Jimmy came to me in June of 1972, he did not know the alphabet. When reciting it, he'd not only mix letters up but he'd omit many of the letters. Jimmy was caught up in memorizing these 26 letters, thus giving him a problem in knowing the letters and their sounds. This is also why he has problems in reading. I have been trying to strip him from memorization and taking the letters and sounds in a mixed-up way and not in chronological order. For example, instead of starting with A is for apple (etc.), we have worked on the letters m, s, d, g, t, f, and h. He still, at this time, does not comprehend H. For example, if I give him the sound for h and ask him what letter it is, Jimmy will reply (on his fingers)...counting the alphabet from A to H...and sometimes forgetting the name for the letter H or how to make the H sign. He is quite confused in this memorization problem.

(Recognition of Sounds): In this test, I mixed up the 26 letters and recited a sound of a letter for him. He in return would write down the sound he heard. Though he did well on this test, he still was in a state of guessing and memorization. He does not comprehend the vowels. He confuses the g and j; s and c; the f and v; the b and d...and has trouble with u, v, w, y, and z.

(Recognition of Word Beginnings): With this test, I gave him a word, and he would write the letters of the first sound he heard. It is the same type of test as the test above except I used a word and not just a letter. The vowel problem comes out more in this test.

(Rhyming Words): Jimmy was on his own in this test. I did not recite any words to him, thus making this test like his first test...that of sight recognition. What he was to do was to circle the word that did not have the same ending as the other two words that were alike. He did fine on this sight test...but as for reading the words, he had a great deal of difficulty. These are first grade vocabulary words. His difficulty in reading was due to him confusing sounds and letters.

(Word Recognition): This is a good reading readiness test for Jimmy. He was given three words, and I recite only one word. From the sounds I give, he chooses what he hears. He did fine, but if you look at the word BALL...he circled the word DOLL...this is because of confusing b and d and not comprehending vowel sounds. He really thought he circled ball.

(Sequence Alphabet): This test requires Jimmy to write the next letter in the alphabet. It took him 10 minutes to do this test. From this test, it will tire him out to start from the letter A to find out what follows the letter T. He still does not know the alphabet in the correct way...meaning sounds in relationship to letters or letters in relationship to order.

(Spelling): I arrange the spelling in three groups. The first 8 words are words Jimmy is familiar with already. His only error here is with the word "bat," which he spelled as "dat." The second group was of six words used in our daily drills. His confusion of vowels is apparent with this group of words. The last group is words we have used but contain letters Jimmy has a hard time comprehending their sounds. Some examples of misspelled words are "bib" for "baby" and "ad" for "egg."

(Evaluation): Jimmy is a willing and cooperative learner. His confusion with the alphabet leads him to other problems though:

1. The alphabet itself he has memorized.

2. He counts the alphabet on his fingers as a child would count to ten on his fingers.

3. He confuses the sounds with the letters.

4. He does not know the names of all the letters.

5. The alphabet problem leads him to trouble with his speech, reading, English, and other related problems.

6. Jimmy will have trouble doing second grade work and is behind in his understanding of first grade work.

*****

This was the beginning of Adversity. Academically, it had made its way into my life. After my mom and dad reviewed the report and talked with the school, my dad pretty much refused to have me held back. The plan was that I would be promoted to second grade, but I would have Ms. Bamer as my primary teacher. Her classroom was a regular-sized classroom with Ms. Bamer's desk in the middle of the room. All of our desks had three sides to them and were placed around the outside walls of the class. We had a carpet area and a sandbox to work on spelling. I would have fifth graders read with me in the hallways. I continued to improve but at a lower rate than my peers. I would get promoted every year to a new grade and get a homeroom teacher, but I would still spend most of my time with Ms. Bamer. I was with my regular class for music, art, gym, lunch, and recess.

During this time, adversity continued to become a bigger part of my life. I was an easy target for other kids to pick on me. Adults were frustrated and not sure how to help me. To make matters worse, my parents had my head shaved, and I was overweight. One of the favorite things kids would say to me was "Wish I had a watermelon." I would get frustrated and found myself occasionally getting into fights. Overall, I was a very compliant and nice kid, but I had to visit the principal's office more than I would have liked to. I was primarily reacting negatively to the other kids picking on me. My struggles continued, and even Ms. Bamer would get frustrated with my dyslexia. In fifth grade, she wrote my mom and said that my oral reading was poor and suggested that if I was struggling with a word, to read it backward so that I might comprehend it the right way. She also said my comprehension seemed fine when I read silently.

Toward the end of fifth grade, Ms. Bamer suggested that I start to spend more time in my regular class to get ready for middle school. I started with math and spelling. I started there because math was one area in which I was doing pretty well. Because of my great memory and willingness to study, I did quite well on spelling "tests." I would memorize the list and almost always got a perfect score even though I couldn't spell while writing. I would find some success.

Middle school came, and I was assigned to Mr. Lawson's class. For the first time ever, I would start a year in a regular classroom. I was excited, but I still felt insecure and worried about how the other students would treat me. I was given a tutor, Mrs. Broadhurst, for two hours a day. We met in a very small, narrow room off the library of Troy Junior High in Avon Lake, OH. She would help with flash cards, read tests, and help me catch up on areas I was behind in. It was a little confusing for Mrs. Broadhurst to have someone for that length of time, and she wrote on the back of my grade card, "Am I supposed to help Jim with the material he has in class or teach him the material he is missing when he is with me?" She decided to help me with the material I had in class, so I wasn't accountable for the material I missed while with her. This would later cause problems due to not knowing things I should have learned.

Even though math was my strength, it was hard to notice this strength when there were so many other problems. In middle school, the math started having more story problems that used dates and times. This made it appear as if I had trouble in math as well, but the math wasn't the problem—reading the story was the problem. As much trouble as I had with reading, writing, and English, it was understandable that my strength in math was missed. I was placed in a math class that would take two years to cover what was normally covered in one. This would put me behind in math all the way through high school.

So here I was in middle school, dyslexic, with a tutor and now in a math class that did not highlight this actual academic strength. It was time for me to continue the fight but to do so in a way that I could get positive attention. I needed to find something positive in my life that I could be proud of…something that would bring me happiness. Something for me to have that was mine and that I could be successful at…that would define me and not my disability. Bring on the social awkwardness of middle school and one talent show.

In middle school, things actually got a little easier socially, primarily because of girls. No, the girls didn't like me, but they did divert the attention of the other boys from me a little. It was a relief, but I was still struggling with being accepted and being seen as a regular kid. One way I decided that I could get positive attention was to go out for the school talent show. My family considered me to be uncoordinated and without rhythm, and to be honest, they were correct. I really couldn't hear tones well and didn't have any natural rhythm. However, I did learn to spin a basketball in sixth grade.

My brother, Mike, knew how to spin a ball and could do some tricks. Every time my dad had business people over, he would have Mike spin basketballs for them. At an NBA game, my sisters, Mike, and I each got a basketball as a door prize. I remember all four of us trying to spin the ball in the family room for hours. It took months, but I learned how to keep the ball balanced on my finger. That was the only talent I could think of for the Troy Junior High Talent Show. Looking back now, I did have a talent. It started small, with a boy spinning a basketball at a talent show. If I hadn't taken that chance and taken that moment to find something that would define me, my life might be completely different now. Little did I know at that time that I was going to take my talent and spin my way from LD to becoming who I am today—Jim "Basketball" Jones.

My first show ever was in seventh grade, and I spun one ball and did some simple ball-handling drills. I enjoyed the attention I received from spinning a basketball, so I continued to practice. In eighth grade, I spun two balls, and in ninth grade, I attempted to spin three balls for the talent show. (Middle school in Avon Lake went through ninth grade at that time.)

Over the summer between my ninth and tenth grade years, I attended a basketball camp in Wooster, Ohio. One night the camp held a talent show to keep the campers busy before lights out. I did my talent show routine, and everyone was impressed. The next day a world-famous ball handler, "Crazy" George Schauer, was scheduled to appear at the camp. The camp director asked if I would show George my basketball routine and tricks. George was so impressed that he invited me to come and perform with him at the Cleveland Cavaliers games. Opportunity had begun to knock at my door.

The Class that Changed Everything

By high school, I was no longer being tutored but still had numerous "special" classes. One of these classes was called Reading in the Real World and was taught by Mrs. Irene Schuster.

This was *the* class that changed everything for me regarding reading.

It was my senior year, and time was running out for me to improve my reading skills before graduation. Mrs. Schuster broke down reading by the number of words read per minute and, even more specifically, to how many eye movements or "eye fixations" per line of text. This was a new way of looking at reading that allowed me to set numeric goals and monitor my own progress. It also enabled Mrs. Schuster to discover some of my poor reading strategies, some of which were strategies learned in elementary school.

Mrs. Schuster helped me realize I needed to look at more than one word at a time and I shouldn't go back to reread a sentence every time I didn't know a word. I started that class reading only 86 words per minute, which was around a second-grade reading level. I had the slowest reading rate in the class by far. Up to that point in high school, my mom would read me my homework to help me keep up with my classes.

The students in Mrs. Schuster's class would perform countless timed readings and record their progress. The timed readings would be performed while the book was under a machine that would move a light down the page slightly above the reader's normal reading rate. This would help each student keep pace and push them to go faster. It worked well for me. By the end of the class, I was reading nearly 160 words per minute. The class then went one step further by teaching study methods. These study methods would make a world of difference for me when I went off to college.

My high school classes were pretty basic. I didn't take literature, composition, any science past biology, or any foreign language. The one college prep class I did take was accounting. I did well in my classes and worked hard to carry a 3.2 grade point average. I felt good about my grades and was excited to find out I met the school's qualifications for National Honor Society. I found out quickly from the guidance counselor, though, that I didn't take the "real classes" that would justify me being in National Honor Society. Adversity again had made a mark on me. I wasn't willing to give up the fight, and it was this that I used to motivate me to excel in college.

During my high school years, it was hard for me not to feel different from the other kids. They still called me Jimmy, and certain unpleasant nicknames from elementary school would rear their ugly head as well. It was a tough time emotionally for me to try to fit in and see myself as a regular student, even though I had been officially out of the LD program as of tenth grade. I still saw the other kids as being smarter than me, and I lacked self-confidence academically, even with my high grade point average.

I would find myself driving to Redwood Elementary School late at night to dunk a basketball on the nine-foot-high rims. The nets were chain link, and I enjoyed the sound of the metal. I would shine my car headlights on the rim and just pound out my frustrations on those low rims. I felt like a lot of other high school kids who just want to be accepted.

It was at this time my neighbor, Nancy Sobol, came over to ask me if I would help kids learn how to swim at Our Lady of the Wayside group home. It was a home for the handicapped. I soon found out how lucky and fortunate I was and that there were kids much worse off than I was. I had finally found a place where I felt valued and received unconditional love. It was the beginning of many visits to Our Lady of the Wayside and the nursing home across the street. I would go and entertain them with my juggling and basketball spinning. They would laugh and be inspired. Seeing people being affected positively by me started replacing the emptiness I had always experienced because of feeling so different. I recruited other kids to come join me. Some would sing or play the piano, and others would juggle with me. It became a little show, but most importantly, it was a way for me to shine and to show my love for others.

To make my high school years even more difficult, my parents divorced my sophomore year, and my dad's company went bankrupt. My dad moved out of state, and my mom had more things to worry about than just my education. However, she still found time in her busy schedule to read to me when I couldn't keep up in a class. She would also fill out every college admissions application, student financial aid, and government grant forms that I needed for me to attend college. She was the rock that I found I could always lean on when I needed help.

I took the ACT and didn't do that bad. My composite score was 17, which was pulled up greatly by my 25 in math. My English score was only 10, which meant that 90% of the kids taking the ACT did better than I did. My natural science score wasn't much better at 14, but my social studies helped with a 19. My school of choice was Bowling Green State University, but my ACT score put me in the bottom quarter of entering freshman. I was accepted by Bowling Green State University based on my high school class rank and grade point average. It didn't matter to me how I got in. I got in and was heading off to college!

Toward the end of my senior year, my mom wanted to look up Ms. Bamer and send her a letter telling her how well I had done in high school. She had since gotten married, but my mom found her and wrote a nice letter and sent my senior picture with it. One of my favorite things I received from my high school graduation was a letter back from Ms. Bamer (now Mrs. Day). She wrote, "Great to hear from you. You have grown to be a handsome young man. I remember you so well and I am proud of all your accomplishments…. I hope I don't offend you, but it is so hard for me to believe what you accomplished because you struggled so much in elementary school. I will frame your mom's letter and your senior picture and read it to my class at the beginning of each year."

I had fought the fight. I hadn't let dyslexia define me. I rose to meet one of my greatest challenges and defeated it. I had found a talent and something I enjoyed doing. Yet adversity hadn't let me go. I still had a fight and called college, but I was determined to succeed.

College Honors

Going off to college scared me. I was intimidated by almost every aspect of college at the beginning. My first class would be on the seventh floor of the library. Even going into a library was scary, primarily because I had no clue how they worked. On the first day of college, I worked my way to the seventh floor for my first college class, English 110.

English 110, as everyone who has been in college knows, is the course that makes or breaks a person. It is the class that causes students to drop out of college and not return. Here I was in the middle of the class on the first day of college. I was in the one place that so many people thought I wouldn't be. College. I was staring it straight in the face. This class was my worst subject, and to make matters even worse, I had to pass this class to stay at Bowling Green.

The graduate assistant teaching the class, or as I refer to him, "Mr. College," had long hair and a smiley face t-shirt on. He swung his hair back and, with a smile on his face, began to explain to all of us about how half of the class would not pass the course, and when they retook the class, another half would fail. The teacher continued the doom and gloom of passing the class for a whole hour while I calculated in my head that if those numbers were true, I didn't have a chance of passing. I reached for my book bag to leave and give up. However, my chair made an awful noise that made everyone stop and look at me. I didn't want to embarrass myself in front of the other students, so I put my book bag down and figured I could give college at least an hour before quitting. I knew that no one had expected me to go to college, and no one would even bat an eye if I failed—excluding my mom. At the end of the class, the teacher explained that the university had a writing lab in Hayes Hall for people that wanted extra help. If a student needed help beyond the lab, he would be glad to help as well. I decided that if people were willing to help me, I could at least accept their help and see how it turned out.

I stayed in school and started receiving an F on every paper. I continued to go to the writing lab and ask my teacher for help. I just didn't have any experience in writing. Not only was my spelling poor but I really didn't have a clear understanding of grammar. So much of my education to this point was to help me with my reading problem that I never learned grammar. I also knew if I could somehow pass English 110, I would still have to deal with English 112. Fear started to mount as the semester came to the end and I had not written a single passing paper. To be specific, I had received 15 straight F's.

My only chance to pass the class was to somehow pass the proficiency. It was time to write in a little blue book for over an hour and see what happened. My other three classes were going well, and the only possible problem in my first semester would be English 110. Back at home with my mom, we opened the grade card together and both cried. I did it! I had passed English 110 and had received all A's in my other classes. I had made it through the first semester and only had seven more to go. I had again overcome adversity.

During my second semester, the English courses continued, and as "Mr. College" had explained, freshmen had to take English 112, which was now for a letter grade and not pass/fail. Again, I went back to Hayes Hall to the writing lab, and again, I was still failing every writing assignment. I would find solitude in the recreation center practicing my juggling and basketball spinning, and one day I met someone who would change the way I would write—someone who had crossed my path and could help me understand how to create a well-written paper. I met a friend—someone who had the same talent as me with juggling! My one talent that had made me successful, that defined me, had led me to this person!

We practiced tossing juggling clubs back and forth, and while talking, I found out that he was working on his graduate degree in English. He was Chinese but was studying English to return to China to teach English. Opportunity had knocked again, and this time I used it to ask for help. After all, didn't I ask for help my entire life, especially when it came to my academics? I jumped and took the opportunity to ask this friend from China to help me learn how to write. As we juggled, I would learn what was expected from me in English 112 and how to write a five- paragraph paper. Going into the proficiency, though, I still had not passed one weekly writing assignment. So once again my only chance was to pass the proficiency. It was another anxious time as my mom and I anticipated the arrival of the next set of my grades to be delivered in the mail. When we opened the grade card, to both of our surprise, we saw a wonderful, awesome grade of "C." I had done it again! I had made it through the first year of college and, most importantly, was finished with English.

I had three more years at Bowling Green, but most of the subjects were in business and more number based than word based. This made things easier for me. I tried to take classes as pass/fail that were not my forte so that I could have more time to study for my business courses.

I had found a rhythm for studying. My peers now regarded me as the "smart kid," and this fueled my drive to always work hard at studying. I would leave in the morning for a class and not return to my room until the last session ended. In between classes, I would go to lounges in the girls' dorms to study. I knew I could study there without getting bothered by others. The study habits learned from Mrs. Schuster's class were really paying off now. I had a study routine that reduced the anxiety of "never being done studying" that most people experience in college. I attended every class no matter how cold or windy it was. I sat in front or near the front of the class, took detailed notes, and participated in class discussions. As I sat in class, I also realized that what the professor made look easy in class would be more difficult later when I tried to apply it. I figured I better try my hardest to learn the material in class. I also needed a head start, so I would at least preview the chapter before class, if not read it.

All math assignments would have to be done before class so I could find out what I was doing wrong. I knew I couldn't learn from my mistakes if I didn't take the time to make the mistakes beforehand. This enabled me to learn more in class and helped me keep up with the rapid pace of college.

Each week I would read every chapter that was assigned for that week. It was impossible to read all the chapters at once for the final. My reading rate was approximately 160 words. I could only read about 10 pages per hour from a college textbook. This would mean I would have to budget roughly four hours per chapter per class for reading, so I would schedule and plan for 20 hours of studying per week.

Most of the weeks, I was able to beat the clock and save time. Each chapter was highlighted in orange highlighter, which made the text jump out on the page for me. I would reread the highlighted portions up to five times before the test. Each time I could get through it faster so that eventually the shade of the highlight and the boldfaced word would be enough for me to see it and know what it meant. I would take out my notes from class and reread them at least three times before the test. On test day, my routine was to go over the material one more time, juggle in front of a mirror with three rubber balls, open my top drawer and throw the balls in, and slam the drawer shut. I would grab my book bag and walk briskly to the test. As the test was handed to me, I would say to myself, "How dare you test me! It's my time to show off." Even with a slow reading rate, I was able to finish most tests before others. I had reviewed and reread so much, I could tell you what page the answer was on and the shape of the highlight. Most tests would come back with scores over 100% when the curve would be factored in. The BGSU grading scale was A, B, C, D, and F, without pluses or minuses, which made life easier for me. I could accumulate high exam scores during the semester and relax during finals, needing only 50% to keep an A.

During my four years at BGSU, I achieved the following honors:

- Phi Eta Sigma Freshman Honorary

- Beta Gamma Sigma Honorary – Top 5 % of Class

- Who's Who Among Students in American Universities and Colleges

- Dean's List – 6 times

- Outstanding Finance Student Award

- Outstanding Graduating Senior – Finance

- Wall Street Journal Award – One of the Country's Best Business Students—name listed in *The Wall Street Journal*

I received five job offers before I graduated and decided to pursue a career in finance. I eventually took a job in Columbus, Ohio, that allowed me to obtain an MBA from the Ohio State University. I continued to work in the corporate world until my late twenties. As time went on, I eventually realized that my greatest gift was working with people, and I was being driven back to performing.

A-ha moments can be big or small. Mine happened one day when my daughter's kindergarten teacher asked me to come in and juggle for the class. It was in this moment that I realized how much I missed performing and making others smile and laugh. I took a "shot," and it wasn't long after this that I sent out letters to other local schools to see if there was an interest in my program.

This "shot" I took, which was all based off of a tiny moment in my life when I performed at a middle school talent show, created an opportunity. It was one of the most monumental days in my life— you know, the one that most of us can relate to and remember, the one that is engrained in our memory, when life says, "You have worked hard. Here is your chance."

A principal and a school came into my life and changed it forever. Immaculate Conception Catholic School in Port Clinton, Ohio, called to book my assembly program. Sister Rita Kramer was so impressed with my presentation and my willingness to share my story that she emailed eighty other Catholic schools about me. She told me, "Jim, this is what you are meant to do. The Lord is working his magic through you."

That was 20+ years ago, and I'm still going strong as Jim "Basketball" Jones. I have learned a lot and have experienced a lot of magical moments over the years.

Remember, you are the best you ever born and you are worth the fight! Don't ever give up. We all learn over time, and we all learn differently. The key is to keep learning! Keep investing in yourself by continually reading and learning. Find who you are, and reflect on life's moments—and don't blink. Life is unforgiving. Don't miss that moment, that time in your life when you make a choice to find a talent that defines who you are. We all have talents; we are given them as gifts, and they can emerge at any given time. It can be as simple as wanting to bring positivity into your world and being in a talent show. It is that moment that I want you to have, this one thing that you created for yourself and that one moment that changes your life forever.

You may wonder how do you do that. How do you overcome your challenges? When you are in the darkness of adversity, how do you look out and see a ray of light that will lead you to where you are supposed to go? The next section of this book will include the lessons I learned, the words that became who I was to get me through those challenges. Keep reading and keep walking with me as we go back on my journey and reflect. Invest your time in this walk with me. Find one lesson, one word that can turn your life around so you can face adversity with the power to overcome.

Before we continue our walk, though, we must look at the word adversity. Adversity came into my life when I was just a little boy, in many forms and in many ways. It is a part of everyone's life. It is a part of yours.

Adversity
Webster defines adversity as a "state, condition, or instance of continued difficulty or adverse fortune." Note that by definition, "adversity" is not permanent, but a state or instance of difficulty. This is good news.

Our challenges will pass. The question is, how will the challenges leave us when they are gone? Will we be stronger and better, or will we be beat up and devastated? The reality is that we don't get to choose what adversity we'll face in life, but we do get to choose how we adapt. How will we fight back when life knocks us down? We can control how we choose to think and respond to our adversity.

Remember, everyone will face adversity, setbacks and challenges. As my best friend, Shawn Reilley, says, "No one goes through life undefeated." Life will be tough and knock you down, but those challenges can make you stronger and lead you in a better direction.

When people face adversity, the problem isn't always that they give up. The message that adversity continuously sends can cause the problem. It can become your identity and limit what you can accomplish. That limiting view attaches to our backs like a parachute as we run through life, holding us back.

This reminds me of a story I read about research done on the New York Marathon. The NY Marathon has over 50,000 runners annually for its 26.2-mile race through the streets of New York City. Researchers found that the finishing order of the race could be determined at about the 10-mile mark. At the 10-mile mark, they broke the runners down into thirds: front third, middle third, and bottom third. They found that after 10 miles, whichever third a runner was in, this was where they finished the race. The last 16.2 miles didn't determine where runners finished in the race, just the first 10 miles. This is very much like life. We get on a pace, a comfort zone, at an early age, and then we just keep that pace for the rest of our life. I guess the question is, at what age do we determine our pace or place in life?

For most of us, we start to be influenced by environmental clues about who we are and what we are capable of achieving by school age. It's probably rare that the 8th grade honors banquets are significantly different from the senior awards banquets. We get a label or we put a label on ourselves at an early age, and that label becomes a self-fulfilling prophecy of our future success.

But why does it have to be like that? Why do we assume our ability is fixed at such a young age?

Are we buying the story of our challenges and our struggles, or do we believe we can improve and grow? When we see people change and go from the bottom to the top, we make movies about them and call them inspirational. But we all can significantly improve where we are in life by changing our pace (habits) that we live daily. We can change, grow, face adversity, and have hope. We can believe that the power is within us to get to a new level of success. We are not victims of our circumstances, but we are strong enough to fight through adversity to realize our dreams and goals.

There it is—adversity. Now, how did I overcome it? How did I go beyond the darkness and keep striving to be better? Come revisit my past with me and learn. I learned a lot along my journey and hope to share powerful insights that will help you create your story. Through these next pages, you will find strategies to help you live a more meaningful and happy life while you are striving to reach your goals. A truly fulfilling life has to have a purpose and a meaning to it that goes beyond just one's self. Our adversity can be a gateway for us to impact and influence others if we don't give up or settle.

 **What is your action plan? Write your thoughts down here. Remember, thoughts become actions, and actions bring results.**

Write Something! Do Something!

Chapter 2 - Hope

"Hope is being able to see that there is light despite all of the darkness."

– Desmond Tutu

Hope is so powerful. When I was struggling through school, I never thought that I would be a failure in life. It actually never crossed my mind that I would be. The fact that I was in special education and struggled academically would not hold me back. I knew I would be successful one day and would even own my own business. This hope and belief didn't shield me from the realities of my struggles. I was picked on and made fun of frequently in school due to my poor reading and stuttering. I can still hear them calling me names in my head to this day. I remember thinking, *When I own my own business, I'll never hire that kid. He's plain out mean and rude.*

In my mind, I was going to be a successful businessman one day, and that strong conviction gave me hope. But the question is, why did I have this belief, and how did I get it?

Ever since I was little, my mom loved me and took care of me. She provided a stable and safe place to grow up. She invested her time in me and made me always believe that with hard work and determination, I could accomplish anything. I can't thank her enough for all that she did for me.

My dad and I were not close and didn't have a good relationship. He had his own business and worked long hours. He was very close with my brother, Mike, the oldest in the family. I think he had more time available when Mike was little to play with him than when I came along a little over four years later. Mike was very much the son my dad would expect to raise. He was tough and athletic; I think he was born with a six-pack. I was probably born with pudding packs. I wasn't aggressive and really not very tough. I was what my dad referred to as a momma's boy. I don't think this was a compliment, but to be honest, I didn't have a problem being a momma's boy. I loved my mom and I feared my dad, but I really wanted his attention. So when he talked, I listened. I listened because I wanted to be accepted and loved. Adversity began way before I needed to know the letters of the alphabet or learn how to read or before I was labeled dyslexic. The way I could try to overcome it with my dad was to listen. And so I did. And, oh my, did he talk. He loved to tell stories.

The four of us were immersed in stories about success and work ethic. We frequently heard stories about how a person that was at the bottom of the ladder at a business would eventually make it to the top by hard work, determination, great customer service, etc. These stories always had a similar theme: Mess to Success. I grew up on "self-help" motivational material, and those messages became a part of me. I listened to them, and I believed in them. They gave me hope that anyone can start at the bottom of the ladder and climb to the top. My hope came from all of these stories that helped me learn to believe anyone could make it, even people that struggled. My struggles with sounds, letters, and reading were just my mess, but if I worked hard, was determined, and went above and beyond, it would turn into success. I guess I grew up on what Carol Dweck would describe in her book, *Mindset*, as a growth mindset. This growth mindset I developed in elementary school helped me significantly throughout middle school, high school, and college. It gave me hope and allowed me to believe even when so many people couldn't see past my current struggles to see who I could become.

Another way of looking at the power of hope was shared with me by one of the schools I visit as Jim "Basketball" Jones. While visiting Milan Elementary in Milan, IN, I was chatting with one of my favorite principals, Jane Rogers. She shared with me an interesting insight that goes along with having hope and believing.

Upon entering the school, Jane and I began talking, and she showed me a new way of thinking: "Jim, put past, present, and future into the following equation that makes the most sense to you: **My _____ + My _____ = My _____.**"

I thought about it and said, "My past plus my present will equal my future."

She said, "That's great. There isn't a wrong answer." Then Jane said, "Can I show you another way to look at it? How about My Past plus My Future equals My Present."

I said "WOW, I like that!" Our past got us to where we are today, but our view of the future will determine what actions we will take today. If we don't believe in our future or we have no hope for the future, we won't be very active in the present. Since the only action we can take is in the present, our view of the future is critical in determining our actions in the present.

When I relate Jane's insight of the Past, Present, Future equation (what is referred to as "The Equation of Hope") to my life experiences, it really seems to make sense. I always believed in my future, so I didn't mind working in the present because I had hope. If someone doesn't have a good outlook on their future or they have been told they have no future, it wouldn't surprise me that their present-day actions aren't that great.

Have hope. Even if you are struggling, know there is light in all the darkness. It's called HOPE. I have hope in your future, my friend.

What is your action plan? Write your thoughts down here. Remember, thoughts become actions, and actions bring results.

Write Something! Do Something!

_____

_____

_____

_____

_____

_____

_____

_____

_____

_____

_____

_____

_____

_____

_____

_____

_____

_____

_____

_____

Chapter 3 – Believe

"Believe in yourself! Have faith in your abilities!
Without a humble but reasonable confidence in your own
powers, you cannot be successful or happy."

– Norman Vincent Peale

You have to believe that something good will come out of your adversity, that you are deserving of something good, and that you have a special gift. You need to believe that miracles can happen, that love exists everywhere, and that you can overcome adversity and challenges.

Believing is powerful. My wife, who truly trusts in the word "believe," gave each of our boys a little wooden block with the word "Believe" carved in it when they went to college. Why? Because she knows that the comfort of home, the tiny whispers of "you can do it if you believe" will not be as strong when they go off to college. Mom isn't there every day to remind them of this. They are headed into a new world—one that can be filled with adversity and challenges as they grow older and become adults. It can be tough, and she wants them to have a little reminder right on their desk to help them. She wants them to hear her, to hear that whisper as they look at the word, and for that word to always be there giving them the power over adversity and challenges—to always "Believe."

Some people don't believe they are worthy or capable of success. This type of logic stems from a false belief that we are born with all of our talents, abilities, and intelligence at birth and that a person's ability is fixed and can't be altered or significantly improved. It's an "If you got it, you got it, and if you don't, you don't" type of thinking.

This is not my mindset at all. I believe we all can improve and grow over time with effort and deliberate practice. Our abilities, talents, and intelligence are not fixed but malleable. When I hear people talk about their shortcomings, I hear this fixed mindset: "I'm not able to do that," "I'm not smart enough to do that," "I'm not athletic enough to do that," and so on. But what they are missing is the belief that they can grow and improve to be able to accomplish "that." Their statements are just one word short of changing from a defeatist attitude to an optimistic attitude: YET. When you add the word "yet" to your statements, you are adding hope and the belief that you can improve and grow over time. You're not there yet, but you can get there. That is a powerful belief!

Carol Dweck wrote about the problems with fixed mindsets in her book, *Mindset*. Individuals that believe their abilities are fixed tend not to take on challenging tasks. Challenging tasks help us grow and improve, but when you have a fixed mindset, you believe that challenging task will reveal your permanent shortcomings. If you can't do it, , why try? Another big issue with having a fixed mindset is that you are always trying to prove and validate your worth compared to others. On average, people with a fixed mindset tend to put other people down so they can feel worthy and superior. If you have a fixed mindset and a person can do something better than you today, then you believe they will always be better than you. So it's natural for people with a fixed mindset to try to hold other people down or below them in order to feel good about themselves.

Going back further then Carol Dweck's work, I enjoy the ideas and theories of Martin Seligman, the father of positive psychology and author of many books. In his book, *Learned Optimism*, Martin explains the difference between optimistic and pessimistic people, which seems very similar to growth and fixed mindsets, in my opinion. Optimistic people see defeat or life's hard knocks as temporary setbacks. They believe these setbacks aren't their fault and are just circumstantial or bad luck. Therefore, they are unfazed by setbacks and perceive them as a challenge to try harder. A pessimistic person takes defeat and life's hard knocks as more permanent and believes that the setbacks will undermine everything they do and are their fault. Martin labeled this pessimistic belief with three P's: permanent, pervasive, and personal. Pessimistic people believe defeat or setbacks are all of these things. An example could be getting a bad grade. A pessimistic person getting a bad grade will feel they are dumb; they will never learn it, and they will eventually fail the class. An optimistic person looks at a bad grade and thinks they need to study more, ask for help, and just work harder in the class to improve. Another example could be a rejection when asking someone out on a date. A pessimistic person will believe that they aren't lovable and will never find someone. An optimistic person will see it as a sign they should try to improve themselves and ask again. They might get a haircut and change their outfit before asking again. If still rejected, they might add cologne and buy flowers, and then ask again. If still rejected, they will figure out they might just be asking out the wrong girl. They believe the right one is out there; it might just take time to find that person.

This helps us understand why some people don't overcome challenges but are devastated by them. There is power in believing if—and only if—we "believe" we can improve and grow and that all challenges are only temporary setbacks. I believe in you, my friend.

 **What is your action plan? Write your thoughts down here. Remember, thoughts become actions, and actions bring results.**

Write Something! Do Something!

_____

_____

_____

_____

_____

_____

_____

_____

_____

_____

_____

_____

_____

_____

_____

_____

_____

_____

_____

_____

_____

Chapter 4 – Why

*"He who has a **why** to live for can bear almost any **how.**"*

– Friedrich Nietzsche

Your purpose will fuel your passion and direction. We need energy to accomplish our goals and dreams, and this is what a strong purpose will give you. The desire to keep striving and working even when things get tough comes from your passion, what a lot of people call your "why." Take time to think about why you really want to accomplish this goal. Why is it important to you? If you don't have a really strong reason why you want to accomplish something, then you will probably quit once you encounter some resistance. Our passion is what drives us to fight through the resistance and overcome the obstacles we face.

Michael Jordan played basketball with passion and at an unbelievably high level. It was almost like he mustered up a superpower for each and every game. He could have lost some games, but he was a fierce competitor every time he stepped out on the basketball court. Why?

When he was asked how he found the energy to play every game with that level of competitiveness and energy, Michael would say, "At every game, there's a kid that has never seen me play or will ever see me play again. I play that hard so that kid will know what type of player I am."

Another story I remember hearing from the motivational tapes growing up was about a factory worker at a stamping plant. This one worker's parts turned out better and with significantly fewer defects than those of the other workers at the factory. The factory manager wanted to know his secret to making consistently high-quality parts hour after hour, day after day. How did the guy mentally do it without getting bored and losing focus? The guy looked at the manager and said, "These parts eventually become part of a bike's brake. Every day, I don't think of making metal parts but about the kid riding the bike. I don't come into work to make metal parts; I am motivated to come to work to make sure what I do will keep a kid safe. I come here to save kids' lives by making great brake parts.

How we decide to define why we are doing something changes how we actually perform our task. These stories have stuck with me in my career as Jim "Basketball" Jones. I have a similar mindset and purpose when I perform. I know in every audience there is a kid that needs me that day. That kid needs a hug, a moment to be in the spotlight, some laughter, or just to feel loved. My purpose for every show is to find that kid and give them what they need. When I look at what I do like that, I never have trouble performing with a high level of energy and awareness. A show is never bigger than one kid and one moment.

Here's a story that to this day gives me a chill. I don't really know how it happened, but stories like this one keep me motivated to do school assemblies. I was presenting a teacher in-service, and I shared with the teachers that schools frequently comment on the kids I pick during my assembly. They say they don't know how I do it, but I pick the right kids that really needed a positive moment. I love hearing this comment because it means I am fulfilling my purpose for why I do school assemblies.

After the teacher talk, we gathered for an assembly with the fifth graders. Five hundred fifth graders sat on the gym floor with the teachers in chairs to the side. I had 75 kids up along the sideline of the basketball court to play the final round of Simon Says. As I walked to mid-court to start the game, I noticed a boy in the crowd sitting on the floor. Even though there were kids all around him, I felt like he was all alone. He had an awkward presence to him. A sadness. I said to him, "I don't know why, but I like you, and you need to play. Go in and be part of the final round of Simon Says." He got up and joined the game. He made it all the way to the final two players. There was a great excitement in the crowd because the final one standing would win an autographed Jim "Basketball" Jones basketball. He lost, and I sighed. As he was walking back to his seat, I stopped him and said, "I like you, my friend, and I don't know why, but you need a basketball. Here's a basketball from me, and remember, I like you, my friend."

After my assembly, teachers came up to me crying and said, "You had to know. Someone told you about that boy."

"No, what do you mean?" I asked.

"That boy lost his father last week, and you just picked him out of 500 kids to give him a ball. If any one of our students needed that today, that boy needed it."

Our purpose will fuel us as we do our best and will help us to reach new levels. But you have to find your "why," your purpose, in order to energize yourself daily. Walt Disney understood the importance of this concept, and he very clearly defined Disney World's purpose while communicating it to all of their cast members. Disney's purpose is to make people happy. This purpose is taught, reinforced, recognized, and rewarded. Disney has empowered their employees to make decisions on a daily basis with one objective in mind: "Make people happy." Disney's purpose is more important than an employee's job. If a guest needs help or to be shown where an attraction is in the park, an employee will leave their post to guide them. Along the way, they will find other ways to make them happy. They'll ask them about other activities they plan to do at the park and give them suggestions on how they can do that best, and they'll ask about their family, where they are from, or how the stay is going.

Having hope and believing in your future will get you started, but developing a strong purpose (why) will power you to go after your goals and dreams. If your *why* isn't strong enough, as soon as you reach some resistance or some adversity, you will quit. If you have established a clear and powerful *why*, you have made a strong commitment to accomplish the task, goal, or dream regardless of the adversity you are facing. What's your reason, your why, my friend?

 **What is your action plan? Write your thoughts down here. Remember, thoughts become actions, and actions bring results.**

Write Something! Do Something!

early in the morning from my home in Toledo, Ohio, to Cleveland to support my mom on her special day. On the way back to Toledo, I received an unexpected call from my mom.

"Where are you?" she frantically blurted out. "I am off the highway with a flat tire."

Thankfully, I was just a few miles behind her and was able to drive to her and change the tire. While I was changing the tire, she said, "I really hope this isn't a sign of how the rest of my retirement is going to go."

Without even looking up, I immediately said, "I am sure *it is* a sign of how your retirement is going to go. That's for sure."

"Jimmy, what do you mean? This can't be a good sign!" Mom replied.

"Mom," I said, "it's a *great* sign. The fact is, in life, we sometimes get a flat tire. Things aren't perfect. Life is full of challenges. But today when you got a flat tire, you were very lucky. What's the chance that you would get a flat when your son, who lives two hours away, was only two miles behind you? Not only that, now that we've met up again, let's take this as a sign we should go have some coffee together and spend more time visiting. How many people could be as lucky as you? If your retirement continues to go like this, you will have the best retirement ever." I had turned a negative into a positive.

Growing up in special ed classes never stopped me from coming into school with a great attitude and being happy. I had my down days and I got angry when kids picked on me, but overall, I was a happy kid. I had good thoughts going through my head, and those thoughts stemmed from my belief that I could learn over time. I would improve. I was born to do well in life. It seemed like a mess, but all the ups, downs, highs, and lows were going to make me stronger so I could find success. It would happen.

It's hard to stay inflated when life throws a bunch of challenges at you. Sometimes it seems like life can be unforgiving, but staying positive is critical to not spiraling downward. It is amazing how poorly a basketball will perform with just a little air let out of it. We perform poorly as well when we are deflated.

It reminds me of when I was little and had the chance to see the Harlem Globetrotters perform at the Richfield Coliseum near Cleveland, OH. I loved watching the Globetrotters; I always wanted to be Meadowlark Lemon. During the game, the Globetrotters would sneak a flat ball into the game and give it to the referee. He would try to bounce the deflated ball and trip over it when it flattened on the ground in front of him. Every time I saw the Globetrotters, I would laugh at that stunt they played on the ref.

It's the same with you! If you are deflated or down, you will perform at a lower level than if you are up and positive. It is how we choose to think that makes the difference. There is research showing that positive emotions are frequently accompanied by fortunate outcomes, like a longer life, a healthier life, more friends, etc. Frequently, people think that positive circumstances will beget positive emotions, but there is research showing the benefits of positive emotions despite the circumstances. One study observed a group of nuns living similar lives and looked into the journals of the nuns. It found that the nuns that expressed positive emotions more frequently and more intensely in the journals lived longer than the nuns that didn't.

The body and mind are tied together. If we stay inflated and express more positive emotions, it will improve our health. On the other hand, negative emotions or a lack of positive emotions will hurt our health.

So how do we stay inflated in order to be at our peak performance?

Wake up each morning and take a deep breath, happy to have another day on this great planet. Cultivate a sense of gratitude for your family and friends. Learn to love where you live. Take time to smell the roses and enjoy the people that are important to you. Never get too distracted with the details that you lose sight of what is truly important. Always look for the good in your challenges.

I find that people who are nice are usually people who are also happy. Grumpy people aren't always nice to others, because they are too worried about their own problems. If you are having a bad day, try to be kind to others, and see if that will change things for you. Smile at someone, listen to a friend, hold the door open for a stranger, make people laugh, call someone you haven't talk with in a while, send a card to a friend, etc. If we are feeling deflated, sometimes when we start to give to others (inflate others), we can pump ourselves up. If none of these ideas work, you can try skipping. Seriously, have you ever seen someone skipping and said, "There goes another sad person"? Actually, the act of skipping will naturally get your body releasing endorphins, and you will start feeling better. Hey, if it doesn't work, at least you have burned some calories.

Being in special ed wasn't the only issue I had to deal with growing up. Going back into my story, my parents were financially successful until about 6th grade, when they had to declare bankruptcy. Then, four years later at Thanksgiving, my dad announced that he and my mom were getting a divorce. He stayed with us until Christmas Eve of that year before joining his new family on Christmas Day. That month that he stayed home was the longest time I remembered him being home with us in years. Being the youngest of four and not the oldest son, I was usually on the short list of his attention anyway. My dad being gone most of my younger days was my normal, so him being around for a solid month was odd. When he left Christmas Eve to be with his new family, it was a challenging moment. I think we four kids were more worried about mom than anything else. I obviously had a lot going on in my life with school, spinning basketballs, and now a bankrupt and split family. I wasn't always happy; I had many reasons to be sad. But I looked for happiness and found it when Nancy Sobol asked me to perform my basketball tricks at Our Lady of the Wayside.

I found my outlet, my niche, that made me happy. I loved being around and working with people! It is really hard to be deflated when you are giving to others, because the feeling of helping others will pump you up.

Stay inflated, and find happiness. It can be simple or complex. Just feel and express positive emotions, my friend.

Our attitude determines our beliefs, which will determine our actions—good attitude, good actions, good results. Remember, my friend, to choose your attitude because it will lead directly to your results.

 **What is your action plan? Write your thoughts down here. Remember, thoughts become actions, and actions bring results.**

Write Something! Do Something!

_____

_____

_____

_____

_____

_____

_____

_____

_____

_____

_____

_____

_____

_____

_____

_____

_____

_____

_____

_____

Chapter 6 – Thoughts Are Real

"A man becomes what he thinks about most."
– Earl Nightingale

Who is the person you talk to most? The one person you share everything with, even your deepest feelings and apprehensions, is yourself.

Our thoughts are real. Self-talk is a powerful tool in creating our self-concept, which leads to how we act and behave. It's not much what happens to us but how we choose to think about it or react to it that matters. We have a little computer in our head that is constantly recording our thoughts and feelings. This little computer is called our subconscious mind. It won't judge or filter our thoughts; it will just record them and use them when needed. If we want to have an abundant life, we have to take control of our thoughts and what we are putting into our heads. If we put good stuff in, we will get good stuff out. If we put bad stuff in, we will get bad stuff out. Garbage in, garbage out!

How we think is not just important but may be the *most* important element in determining our success and our happiness. As Zig Ziglar would say, "Some people have a bad case of stinking thinking." They get in the habit of negative thinking, which begets negative results. Another way Zig talked about our thinking is this way: "You are what you are and where you are because of what went into your mind. But the good news is, you can change what you are and where you are by changing what goes into your mind." How we program our minds with thoughts and self-talk will influence how we live and experience our lives.

Here is the flow of how our *Thoughts* lead to our *Results:*

> **Thoughts → Feelings → Behaviors/Actions → Habits =**
> # Results
> *Thoughts lead to feelings, feelings lead to behaviors/actions, our actions lead to our habits, and our habits will produce our results.*

Our thoughts are created from what we hear, what we see, and our specific experiences. All three of these things lead us to our thoughts, and it is these thoughts that will determine our feelings. Based on our feelings, we decide on what actions to take or not take. These actions or lack of actions will lead to our results. Then the cycle repeats over and over again. But our continued results start to reinforce our initial thoughts, which help determine our beliefs. These beliefs fast track our actions with not much thought from us, leading to a sort of self-fulfilling prophecy. This process, once repeated, becomes our habits, and our habits will determine our results.

It's true; our actions are coming from our thoughts, which have been accumulating in our subconscious since we were little. Drastic changes in behavior often require drastic changes in thinking. However, most people look at undesired behavior and try to change it without looking deeper to discover what thoughts and beliefs are driving that behavior. We can't change the behavior permanently, though, unless we change the underlying beliefs that support it.

Thoughts are real and they play a huge part in our success, happiness, and mental health. Mindfulness training has been helpful for a lot of people because it creates a space between their thoughts and their actions. We need to remember that it's okay to have a thought. Thoughts are neither right or wrong. It's the actions those thoughts drive that is important. If you can change how you think about your thinking, you can change your life, my friend.

 **What is your action plan? Write your thoughts down here. Remember, thoughts become actions, and actions bring results.**

Write Something! Do Something!

_____

_____

_____

_____

_____

_____

_____

_____

_____

_____

_____

_____

_____

_____

_____

_____

_____

_____

_____

_____

_____

_____

Chapter 7 – Respond Instead of React

"E + R = O; an Event plus your Reaction or Response will equal the Outcome."

– Jack Canfield

E + R = O is a mindset. It's a way of thinking about how events lead to outcomes. We don't have control over the events in our life, and not all events are equal. Everyone's life is different, and some people have been granted more privilege or resources to deal with events than others. We have a choice to either "react" or "respond" to any event that happens in our lives. If we react, our reactions tend to be impulsive, on autopilot, and done without thinking. These reactions might feel good in the moment but do not produce positive or productive results. When responding, our actions are intentional, purposeful, and skillful. Responding allows us to grow and improve. We are tackling the challenge with purposeful action that will most likely improve the outcome. Responsiveness also has a psycho-logical impact as well, as we tend to be more in control of our emotions and make more appropriate decisions. Hence, regulating our emotions is healthier for us in the long term. The instant "blowing off steam" of reacting creates bad emotions and, over time, will create a negative health effect.

Take the popular phenomenon of road rage for example. Another motorist cuts you off, which, in some cases, is not just bad manners but is potentially deadly. Your immediate *reaction* might involve some creative gesture. But aside from releasing steam, where does this lead? What good does it accomplish? You might get in an accident trying to catch the other motorist; you might, in short, become the same type of driver as the one that sent you into a rage.

But what happens when we replace our reaction with a response? Responsiveness (emotional regulation) might mean collecting one's thoughts and feeling grateful that nothing worse happened. Changing how you think about the event may help you adjust. Instead of thinking that person is rude and an idiot, think that the driver had an urgent crisis that they were rushing to. Just changing how you frame the situation can help you stay calm and learn to respond to the adversity versus reacting to it. This will allow you to get to where you're going and get there in a healthier frame of mind. In the book, *Above the Line,* Urban Meyer explains Tim Kits's philosophy on how to manage what they refer to as the "R – factor," which means how we control our responses to adversity versus just being on autopilot and reacting when challenges arise. Tim teaches that the first step is to "Press Pause" and ask, "What does the situation ask of me?" In my assemblies I have taught students something very similar, "Pause to Think." The important thing is that we slow down to get our mind straight and make positive, productive, and thoughtful decisions and stop reacting impulsively.

React versus respond isn't just applicable to our actions. Perhaps most importantly, the virtue of responding is embedded most deeply in our listening. Most people have heard the term "active listening," but in my experience, this is a misnomer. Put differently, the term understates the most important aspect of listening: patience.

"Patient listening" is caring listening. Patient listening is responsive. Patient listeners are not eager to hear the sound of their own voice. They actually patiently listen to the person speaking then take a moment to think about what they are going to say and then respond.

Another thing that makes listening difficult is that listening is more visual than we often realize. Most listening is done with the eyes as well as the ears. There is hard science behind this observation, and the social sciences support it as well.

Light moves faster than sound, so our brains receive signals from light before the sound waves arrive. We determine what the person is saying before we actually hear their words. This process is so fast we don't even realize we are doing it. I believe we would all be better listeners if we practiced listening with *patience* and empathy.

Being dyslexic, processing sounds and syllables takes a little longer for my brain to organize and put into words than normal. Sometimes I have a hard time even placing the syllables into recognizable words. This has created a challenge in my life that I have had to overcome in order to reach my goals. I don't use it as an excuse for why I can't do something, but I respond to the challenge by intentionally looking at the person's mouth that is talking. This allows me the chance to use my eyes to pick up the words by lip reading when I can.

As we move forward by taking actions to reach our goals, challenges will arise. We should address these challenges purposefully and skillfully and not just react to them. If we "press pause" and patiently think about the challenge, we can find a solution to the problem. Remember, my friend, to "Pause to Think" and then respond to your challenge that is confronting you.

 **What is your action plan? Write your thoughts down here. Remember, thoughts become actions, and actions bring results.**

Write Something! Do Something!

_____

_____

_____

_____

_____

_____

_____

_____

_____

_____

_____

_____

_____

_____

_____

_____

_____

_____

_____

_____

_____

Chapter 8 – Personal Success Strategies

"Most people engage in activities that are tension-relieving rather than goal-achieving."

– Brian Tracy

Success is inconvenient and involves some level of productive discomfort. Most people try to avoid being uncomfortable or doing things that are hard or difficult. Randy Pausch, in *Last Lecture*, talks about why there are brick walls around the village. He says, "The brick walls are there for a reason. The brick walls aren't there to keep us out. The brick walls are there to give us a chance to show how badly we want something. Because the brick walls are there to stop the people who don't want it badly enough. They're there to stop the other people."

You have to do the hard stuff that you don't want to do so you can get to do the stuff you really want to do. Everything you want is surrounded by something you don't want. We all want a nice retirement, but it isn't fun saving money every month to afford the retirement we want. We would love to start our own business, but it's hard to take the leap into a new adventure. We all want a fit body, but going to the gym daily is a challenge. What is it that is holding you back from being or becoming the person you want to be? Fight through the road block you have put in front of yourself and becoming the person you want to be. I'm not saying it will be easy, but I am saying it will be worth it. If it was easy, everyone would already have it. Challenge yourself!

In the book, *The 7 Habits of Highly Effective People*, Stephen Covey talks about the victory over self. The first three habits help individuals take control over their own lives: be proactive, begin with the end in mind, and put first things first. Being proactive is about taking the initiative to get things done. Don't sit back and wait for success to find you, but **do something** about it. Take action. Think about who you want to be. Start with your end vision, and ask yourself what you need to do today to get there. Putting first things first is about priorities—work before play—but it is also about focusing on the most important task first. What is the one thing I can do today that will allow me to get closer to my goal? We frequently make a to-do list, but then we start cherry picking the easiest or more enjoyable things on the list to do first, not necessarily the things that will get us closer to our goal. As Brian Tracy says, we tend to do tension-relieving things versus goal achieving. Why? Because doing the other things is easier and less painful. We don't usually do the things we dread, but we have to start to put things first based on what's most important. Make your list then rewrite it to include only the two most important things; work on them until they are done and then go back to your original list and find the next two important items.

Take school for example. Most kids don't like to study and do homework. They would much rather play Fortnite or other video games with their friends. But homework is something that most of them do so they can get to do what they want to do: graduate from high school. But what about the students that decide they can't put up with all the high school drama or workload and choose to drop out? They decide they don't want to do the hard stuff and that school just isn't for them. They think it will be easier to just drop out and not go through the pain of doing what high school is asking for them. Once they drop out, some do go back to school to acquire a GED. But here's the question—what are the life outcomes for people that decide not to stick with high school and drop out? Does going back to get a GED improve their life outcomes?

In the book, *How Children Succeed*, Paul Tough refers to research by economist James Heckman, who compares high schoolers that drop out and go on to get a GED to students that drop out and don't get a GED. In general, Heckman believed IQ to be a significant factor in positive life outcomes before he started his research. He hypothesized that the IQ of dropouts and GED recipients would have been similar and lower than high school graduates. He was surprised to find that students that dropped out and eventually got a GED had similar achievement test and IQ scores as high school graduates. With further study, however, he found out that only 3% of GED recipients were either in a four-year college or had graduated from a four-year college by age 22 versus 46% of high school graduates—a significant difference for kids with a similar IQ.

His research also showed that GED recipients' life outcomes exactly correlated to high school dropouts when comparing income, unemployment, divorce, drug use, and the like. He concluded that GED students, even though they possessed the intelligence to do well in life, lacked psychological traits like persistence, the ability to delay gratification, and follow-through. These traits held them back from achieving the positive life outcomes they were capable of achieving. Heckman explained in one paper, "The GED has become a test that separates bright but non-persistent and undisciplined dropouts from other dropouts."

A person's willingness to stay with a difficult task is significant in predicting their life's future outcomes. Remember, a little bit of productive discomfort is needed in life. Stick with it, and don't shy away from the difficult tasks that will lead to your goals and dreams. What are the most important things you can do today that will help you achieve your goal?

I believe we all have to challenge ourselves to constantly try to improve and grow. Below I have detailed different strategies to help you challenge yourself. I hope these eight little strategies help you in the pursuit of your goals and dreams.

1. Focus on Fundamentals

> *"It's the small things we learn and master*
> *that make the hard things look simple."*
>
> **– Jim "Basketball" Jones**

People's perception of success is often their biggest obstacle in achieving it. For some reason, people feel they will be successful only after they accomplish something grand. This is backward thinking. Don't focus on the big picture so much that it becomes overwhelming. The big picture *is* overwhelming. Success is in the details. Success is a lot of little things done well that add up over time.

UCLA basketball coach John Wooden broke success down into four P's: planning, preparation, practice, and performance. It is these fundamentals that are found in success, which Coach Wooden defines as the "peace of mind which is a direct result of self-satisfaction in knowing you made the effort to become the best of which you are capable." I like this definition of success. It's really about becoming your best and not the best. Everyone who came into contact with Coach Wooden knew he was a proponent of mastering fundamentals rather than flash. Coach Wooden preferred substance over show. He would write out every practice in detail in order to not waste time and to keep his players moving. He knew that his players would only improve with deliberate and intense practice.

Not only did he focus on the details of his practices but Wooden would even teach his players how to properly put on their socks. That sounds crazy, but it wasn't craziness. In Wooden's mind, the small details matter, like having your socks on correctly. If they didn't have them on correctly, they would get blisters, and blisters affect performance. Socks matter. Wooden coached success in the little things. If we focus on the little things, the fundamentals, the large things will take care of themselves.

A concept I came up with to help me focus on the small details and not the big picture is something I call "piece of cake." Piece of cake is commonly used to mean something is simple and/or easy. During my school assembly program, I occasionally ask a teacher why we use the expression "piece of cake" to mean easy. It is always funny to watch them make up an answer. I really don't know the answer either, but I do know what it means to me. Piece of cake means easy because it means to quit trying to eat the whole cake; take it piece by piece. To me, that means breaking it down and focusing on the small fundamentals and not the big picture. This is a simple concept that helps me concentrate on the small pieces that, when put together, will make the whole task.

Kids love to shoot the three-point shot, and so do NBA players. The game of basketball has turned into layup-dunks or three pointers. When I work with kids on shooting, we focus on form and technique, not how far they can shoot. It's hard, though, because the perception is, the farther you can shoot, the better shooter you are, so kids want to shoot as far as possible from the basket. The way to become a great three-point shooter, though, isn't by shooting three pointers, at least until you develop the correct form and strength. Simply practicing rolling the ball off your fingers is a good start. Once you have a smooth roll, then practice hitting a target on the wall using perfect form. The benefit of doing this is you can get tons of reps in without ever running after the ball. Reps are what is important to develop muscle memory. They say it takes 10,000 hours of deliberate practice to become an expert at something, but people want the end result too fast. To become great, you have to fall in love with the process and not the end result. The end result is way down the road; if you don't enjoy the process, you won't stick with it long enough to master the skill. Focus on the small things that will make you great, and place your ego on the shelf. You will master it over time and with deliberate practice if you stick to it and put in the time. Fundamentals are the key, my friend! Focus Daniel-son…

2. Own Your Effort

"Strength and growth come only through continuous effort and struggle."
–Napoleon Hill

Effort is the main ingredient of all success. We can make a great plan and have all the ability in the world, but if we don't take action, something terrible will happen. It's called…nothing. Doing something takes effort and you might fail, but if you do nothing, you are guaranteed to fail to accomplish your goal or task. A lot of us find more reasons why we can't be successful rather than finding a reason why we can be successful. We look at our own ingredients and find faults:, I'm not smart enough, I'm not talented enough, I'm not tall enough, I'm not skinny enough, I don't have enough money, I don't know enough, I'm not funny enough, I'm not pretty enough, etc. Personally, I'm tired of "enough" excuses. You are "good enough" to get started. Zig Ziglar said it best when he said, "You don't have to be great to get started, but you better get started if you ever hope to be great." Working with what you have is better than complaining about what you don't have and doing nothing. You can improve but only if you get started. I tell the kids in my assemblies, "You don't have to be great to TRY, but if you don't TRY, how will you ever be great?"

People worry they don't have enough talent, especially when they see everything everybody else can do. In my opinion, people have a distorted view of other people's talent. Paul Tough, in his book, *How Children Succeed*, says, "We see talent only after the talent has been developed and think the talent is innate or God given. They never account for all the hours it took to develop the talent."

I view talent not as a constant but as something that is constantly growing and being developed. I define talent as the sum of your genes times your environment PLUS learned experiences. Talent is what you can do, so once you learn or improve a skill, you "naturally" become more talented. For example, everyone would agree that LeBron James is talented and has certain gifts his genes have given him. But those genes were *expressed* in an environment immersed in basketball since an early age and developed through relentless effort and deliberate practice. He is even more talented in his 15th year in the NBA than his rookie year. His talent has grown and improved over time due to his effort at perfecting his craft.

Angela Duckworth, in her book, *Grit*, argues that effort is worth twice as much as talent. She writes:

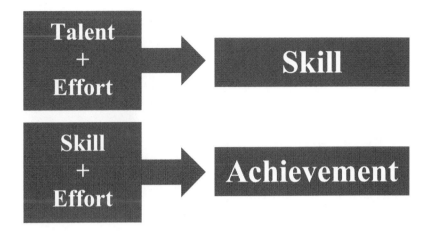

Therefore, you need to apply effort to your current talent to acquire a skill. Then it takes effort to use that skill to achieve—two parts effort' to one part talent.

I use an analogy about making brownies to emphasize the importance of effort in a person's life, primarily because I really like brownies: You can have the best brownie recipe and brownie ingredients in the world, but if you don't mix the ingredients together, your brownies won't turn out. Mixing all the ingredients together takes effort, and it's the same way with you. You have all the right ingredients to be great, but if you don't apply effort to your ingredients, you won't turn out as well.

I had a chance to meet an aspiring young actor, Zack Weinstein, who had a horrible accident and had to really work hard to gain mobility again, let alone pursue his acting career. I met him at a conference that we both presented at. Zack was working hard to make it in the very tough business of professional acting. He was studying acting in college and doing quite well. One day, he and his friends while on a canoe trip, went swimming in a river. One of Zack's friends flipped him over his shoulder. There was a rock they hadn't noticed, and Zack hit the back of his head on the rock. He broke his back and is now a quadriplegic.

After working with his physical therapist for a while, Zack was able to move his arms but didn't have good use of his wrist or fingers. He set a goal of being able to move his wrist—that one simple movement would make his life so much better. As he told me, the ability to move his wrist as a quadriplegic made all the difference in the world to help him become more independent and to give him opportunities to accomplish more.

He worked really hard and improved. Eventually he was up to the challenge of picking up a Skittle from a table and putting it into his mouth. Since he didn't have much feeling in his hands, he would flop his hand down over the Skittles and lift his arm, which would make his fingers close. Then he would turn his arm to see if any of the Skittles were stuck in his fingers. He did this for four hours with no success. His therapist came over and said, "Baby, let me just give you one of the Skittles. You have been working so hard; you deserve a Skittle."

Zack looked at her and said, "It's a damn Skittle, and I will be able to pick up a Skittle or I won't eat a damn Skittle!" As he kept trying, he finally came up with an idea. He said to himself, "Zack, just lick your fingers!" So he licked his fingers and flopped his hand on the Skittles. He then lifted his arm and turned it to see a Skittle! Finally, a Skittle and success. The amount of effort Zack had to expend to finally pick up a Skittle was enormous. That willingness to work hard and fight had allowed Zack to fulfill his acting dream. He has acted on

Criminal Minds, NCIS, Glee, and, most recently, on the YouTube Red hit called *Sing It.*

We own our own effort, and no one has the ability to take it away! Don't worry about the ingredients that you can't control; just focus on the one thing you have total control over: your effort. Apply effort, and you will be surprised what you will be able to accomplish over time. Get started by "doooooing something," my friend.

3. Improve Your Weaknesses

> *"Our strength will soar when we work on*
> *our weaknesses that are holding us back."*
>
> **– Jim "Basketball" Jones**

Most people feel if they just focus on their strengths, they will become the best they can become. They feel if they just use their talents, abilities, and education they can realize their potential. The problem is, we all have weaknesses or behaviors that restrict us from fully using all of our strengths and realizing our true potential.

In a book called *The Flip Side,* Flip Flippen relates the importance of working on your weaknesses: "If you have a very creative person with incredibly low self-control, it's best to tell them to improve the self-control than to instruct them to be more creative." Our weaknesses are like an anchor holding back our strengths. But we enjoy our strengths, and when we are working on our strengths, we feel good about ourselves. When we work on our weaknesses, it's hard, and we don't feel as positive about ourselves. What we need to do is identify what weaknesses are holding us back and develop a plan to improve them. Maybe we can take an online class, hire a tutor, or find a coach or a mentor that can help us improve. If we improve on our weaknesses, our strengths will shine even brighter.

I was visiting a school in Columbus, Ohio, that worked with kids with special needs at all grade levels. The principal shared with me a story about one of their former students, Brendon. He told me when Brendon was about 16, he was living with his mom in Atlanta, Georgia. His mom was getting very frustrated with him and asked his dad if he could take him and enroll him in a school in Columbus, Ohio.

Brendon was making money doing character drawings on the streets of Atlanta. He was messing around with selling other things as well to make it, and his mom was getting concerned. He had not been in trouble yet, but his lifestyle was heading toward trouble quickly. He wasn't listening to her, so she asked his dad to see what he could do for him in Columbus. Brendon had pretty much given up on school. Like me, he had a learning disability, but unlike me, he ran into a few teachers that didn't understand dyslexia. One of his English teachers would mark off one letter grade for every misspelled word. Being dyslexic, I know how hard it is to turn words into letters. Sometimes I even struggle to get the first few letters correct, let alone the whole word. Brendon had enough, and not feeling successful, he dropped out of high school. He loved to draw, and he figured he would just do what he could to make a living drawing. His weakness was holding him back from soaring with his strengths.

Brendon's dad brought him to Marburn Academy in Columbus. At that time, Brendon's hair totally covered his face, and he parted it with his hands if he chose to look at you. The principal and Brendon talked, and the principal asked Brendon if he had ever worked on his art on a Mac. The principal knew Brendon's strength and passion was his art, but he also knew to fulfill the dream of working as an artist, he would need to graduate from high school and probably study art in college. These two things seemed impossible goals at the time, but the principal devised a plan and proposed it to Brendon.

The principal said, "Here's the deal. I will let you work on your art on the Mac for three hours a day if you will work with one of our English teachers for the same amount of time. Is it a deal?" Brendon agreed.

Brendon agreed to work on his weaknesses not only because he was granted the privilege of working on the Mac but also because Marburn Academy was a safe place to learn and improve. Brendon didn't feel judged or inadequate if he misspelled a few words. He was accepted for who he was and where he was academically, and he was asked to improve from there.

And improve he did, both in his English and his art. He began to soar at Marburn Academy. Before he graduated from high school, Brendon won two national art awards and illustrated two books, *The Mountain Song and Lessons Learned* and *A Nest in the Gale*. He received a full scholarship to the Columbus College of Art and Design. He wouldn't have accomplished any of this if some caring people hadn't stepped in and helped him improve his weaknesses.

What is holding you back from being your best? What skills do you need to improve that will help your strengths soar? Improve your weaknesses, my friend.

4. Stretch Yourself

> *"Get out of your comfort zone so you can*
> *get into a learning zone."*
> **– Jim "Basketball" Jones**

We get into our comfort zone and stay there. This isn't uncommon, and I am no different. Doing elementary school assemblies is my comfort zone. I am very comfortable doing that age group and the messages and techniques I can use to make the presentation fun and educational. I even can play fun, happy music that I enjoy during those assemblies as well. But for me to improve, I have to stretch myself to different audiences. For me, that is talking to just adults, primarily in-service training sessions at schools. You would think that is an easier audience since I can lower my energy level and get deeper into the topic, but honestly, it's not something I am as comfortable with. So because I have decided to stretch myself, I need to do more teacher talks. I have seven of them in one month coming up. That will be the most I have ever done in such a small timeframe. This will allow me to improve my adult presentations. The benefits of these talks are all the research I do and knowledge I gain, which makes all my school assemblies even better. It stresses me out, but it also stretches me to grow. Get out of your comfort zone, and try something new. It will stretch you in ways that will allow you to grow and improve.

I have tried to stretch my kids as well. When my daughter, Jennifer, was in the second grade, her mother and I went to a parent–teacher conference. The teacher told us how bright Jennifer was and how impressed she was with Jennifer's writing for a second grader. You would think I would be happy and just shut up—but not me. I looked at the teacher and asked her if she could do me a favor. I said, "The next time you get one of those good papers from Jennifer, could you tell her that she did great but you think she can do better and give the paper back for her to redo?"

You would have thought I asked her to slap Jennifer across the face or something. She looked at me and said, "Mr. Jones, I would never do that to a good student who did exceptional work!" Wow, I didn't see that response coming. I was just asking her to stretch Jen to see how much she could improve her writing. The teacher was comparing Jen to all the second graders she had before and saying she was doing well. I was saying, let's see how well Jen can do by challenging her and asking her to stretch her skills.

The teacher didn't give Jennifer any papers back, and she did well in school. Jen's freshman year of college at Notre Dame, she was very concerned how her work would fit in there. She couldn't wait to turn in a paper and see what she got back. She called me once she got her first paper back and said, "Hey, Dad, I thought you might enjoy what the professor wrote on my first paper: 'This is a good paper but not good enough for Notre Dame. Please correct it and turn it back in."

I yelled, "Wow, Jen, that's great."

Jen said, "You know, Dad, you suck." That girl makes me laugh.

Think about how you can stretch yourself and get out of your comfort zone. This will allow you to develop more skills and hopefully, even more confidence. Stretch yourself, my friend.

5. Be Coachable

"My best skill was that I was coachable. I was a sponge and aggressive to learn."

– Michael Jordan

I was asked the other day, if I could give one piece of advice to someone, what would it be? I thought for a while and said, "Be coachable." It is amazing how many talented people reach a level of success much lower than their potential. I think it has something to do with mindset and ego, like your success is discounted if you had help from other people. There are over seven billion people on the planet, and some people think they need to learn everything on their own. There is so much knowledge we can learn from others that will not only save us time but lift us to higher levels of achievement than if we try to do it all by ourselves.

So here's my little piece of advice: Be vulnerable. It's okay to need help and learn from others. Actually, the most successful people are successful not because they did it all by themselves but because they learned from others. Success leaves footprints, so follow them!

Being coachable isn't just listening to your coach, boss, parents, or spouse; it is actually hearing what they say and then applying it. If you don't apply what they are saying then you won't improve and it is a waste of time.

If you are married and your spouse says, "It would be nice to go to _____ or to do _____," well, why not take action and take your spouse to _____ or do _____. Success leaves clues, coaches give pointers, and spouses drop hints. All we have to do is apply the information and reap the benefits. To improve our chances at success, to improve our role on a team, or to improve our relationship with our spouse, we must take action on information we gain from others. That's called "being coachable."

Needing help isn't a sign that you are dumb or incapable. Seeking and asking for help is a sign of strength and self-confidence. Too many people strut their stuff like they are strong and confident but could grow much more and much faster if they would be vulnerable to learn from others. Being vulnerable is a sign of self-awareness and the capability for self-improvement.

I have found that the most successful people I have met are also the most coachable. They are constantly trying to learn from others, regardless of that person's status or level in life. Coachability and self-awareness are kissing cousins. Actively seek help from others, collecting usable knowledge and applying it.

I hired one of the top speaker coaches, James Malinchak, as my personal coach for my speaking business. Now, I could have eventually figured out the stuff he taught me, but it would have taken years. Why not hire someone with the knowledge and save yourself years of trial and error? He was expensive, but the ideas and strategies I learned from him are still generating income in my business years later. The wasted time would have cost me tons of lost business. Successful people invest in themselves and hire people that have already done what they want to do to coach them.

Being coachable is one of the life skills I learned in special education. My tutors were my coaches, and I was lucky to get one-on-one coaching to help me try to catch up with my classmates. I grew up asking for help because I didn't understand, so it became very normal for me to ask for assistance. Too many people feel if they don't know something or have to ask a question, they are dumb. Imagine if I had that mindset? From my story and my perspective, if I didn't ask something, then I would have continued to struggle, and that didn't seem like a good choice! Why in the world should we know everything? It's impossible. And learning something from someone else doesn't make anyone dumb or beneath them; it just means we are not familiar with something. You can learn it over time with practice if you stick to it. Being coachable is a sign of a learner. Be coachable, my friend.

6. Create Habits

"We are what we repeatedly do. Excellence, then, is not an act, but a habit."

– Aristotle

Our habits are critical in developing the skills and creating the time we need to become successful. There is only so much time in a day, but if we manage our habits and routines, we can utilize that time to grow and improve. Create habits and routines that allow you to utilize your day effectively.

The habits we create not only show our attitude toward improvement but will indicate how long it will take for us to make that improvement. Improvement takes time, and our habits and routines create that time. In the book, *The Compound Effect*, by Darren Hardy, the publisher of *SUCCESS* magazine, the compounding effect of sticking to a task is explained. At first, the results of a small change in our daily routine are hardly noticeable. Then something magical starts to happen as we start to improve on our improvements, and the eventual growth becomes significant. A question Darren asks in his book is, how thick would a piece of paper be if it was folded 50 times? I ask this in my presentations all the time, and the answers range from a few inches to a few feet. The actual answer is almost unbelievable. The thickness of paper would be the from the earth to the sun. It's called geometric progression. The results at first aren't significant but grow exponentially to this huge number just with 50 folds. The same can be true for your growth if you start to take action to improve yourself daily. The long-term growth will compound, but you have to have patience to stick to your daily routine or habit.

What habits are you creating to achieve your goals? It is amazing how a little done over a long period of time makes such a huge difference, like saving money a little at a time, on a regular basis, will add up to a significant amount over time. Time is a powerful compounder of our habits, whether they are good or bad.

What is your goal, and how can you carve out some time in your day to work on it? I hear a lot of people say, "I just don't have enough time in the day to do anything else." I'm sorry to say that this is a victim mentality and frankly isn't true. I enjoy reading Mitch Album, and being close to Detroit, I can also hear him on the radio. While reading his book, *Tuesdays with Morrie,* I found myself saying, "How in the hell does Mitch Album do everything he's doing in his life'" He's on the radio, on *Sports Reporters*, involved with charities, visits Morrie on Tuesdays, writes books, is married, etc. This guy is my idol. He has created habits that allow him to balance his schedule and to work on individual projects at certain parts of the day. He figures it out and doesn't play the victim card of not having enough time.

You can create habits and routines to reach your goal. Break it down and work in small, daily increments. Daily habits pay huge dividends over time. Read 10 pages a day, exercise for 20 minutes a day, cut 100 calories from your daily diet, or write for 10 minutes a day. Create a positive habit today, and watch how it makes a big difference. You can do it, my friend!

7. Compete With Yourself

> *"The greatest competition you will ever face*
> *in your life is competing with yourself."*

– Jim "Basketball" Jones

As author and speaker Brian Tracy says, "People don't fail because their competition is better than them. People fail when they don't apply themselves and don't take initiative to become their best. Failure is, in fact, a failure of action."

My dad would always tell me, "Jim, the only competition in life you will really face is yourself."

Dad wanted me to realize that my success wouldn't be determined by what other people did but what action I took. Dad saw so many talented people stalled by self-doubt or fear of failure. They had ability but didn't apply it, because they constantly compared themselves to other people and worried too much about what other people were doing. We cannot control what other people are doing, but we can control our own decisions and actions. My brother Mike always says, "It doesn't matter what they do but what you do."

My dad knew that with my learning disability, and the crisis of confidence that special education often brings, I was repeatedly getting the message I wasn't as good or as smart as the other students. The teachers wouldn't expressly say that, but it is easy for that kind of culture to weave its way into special ed. Good-hearted teachers, despite their best intentions, conveyed this message in their comments about my work or even their actions when lowering their expectations for me. All of these messages send a message that kids of all abilities pick up on. Kids inherently compare themselves to the other kids in the class. They want to know, am I smart, am I smarter than other kids, am I below average, am I dumb?

In short, this presented me with a crucial decision point: Would I choose to be slow and behind, or would I work to catch up? How I viewed myself would determine how I performed in the classroom. It was sort of a self-fulfilling prophecy.

Put differently, failure is often a failure of the imagination. Its genius is its lack of vision. Take hold of your narrative, your story. Learn to write your story, and make it a success story. This is easy to say but very hard to do when you are in an environment where you are so far behind and everyone knows it. It's like running a foot race and coming in last every time but somehow believing you still will learn to run as fast as other kids someday. The problem is, we naturally compare ourselves to others, and if we don't compare well, we stop trying. If we stop trying, however, the distance between our ability and that of others will continue to grow.

Dad told me all sorts of stories, and most of those stories filled my imagination with zero to hero ambitions. I was the underdog, but I wanted to become the superhero. His stories routinely involved someone working his way up from the bottom to the top by providing great customer service, making an incredible effort, or constantly learning from others. I still remember the story of the bellhop that eventually owned the entire hotel chain. He would say, "Jim, you will see your future when you really believe in your future."

Here's the trick: Dad ignited my imagination. It wasn't long before, at least in my mind, that bellhop was me.

Take hold of your imagination. What story do you want your life to tell? And always remember, you are competing with yourself. Become *your* best, not *the* best. Don't let what other people can do stop you from working on what you want to do. Compete to improve yourself, my friend.

Be Your Best

8. Take a Shot

"I've missed more than 9,000 shots in my career. I've lost almost 300 games. Twenty-six times I've been trusted to take the game-winning shot and missed. I have failed over and over and over again in my life. And that is why I succeed."

– Michael Jordan

That is one of my favorite commercials. "I have failed over and over and over again, and that is why I succeed." So powerful. So many people are afraid of making a mistake that they don't try. They are afraid that they might look dumb, so they give in.

You have to be willing to fail if you are going to take a shot at success. This reminds me of the movie, *Top Gun*, when the tower is yelling at Maverick, "Engage, Maverick, Engage!" At that moment, Maverick is paralyzed with self-doubt and fear as he remembers how he lost control of his plane and lost his best friend in the accident. "No, it's not right," he says. His co-pilot pleads with him, "Get in there, Maverick. Iceman needs you." It's an intense part of the movie as Maverick battles his fears to engage the enemy.

We all have fears. Research says that humans are born with only two fears: the fear of falling and the fear of loud noises. All other fears are learned. You can look at fear as an acronym: False Evidence Appearing Real. We all have to work on getting over our fears.

Success just doesn't happen on its own. Success starts with action; you have to engage success. And when you take that first step, there is a chance you will fall flat on your face. But if you have the correct mindset that you may fall on your face a few times before you find your way, you will eventually become successful.

We worry that one wrong decision will ruin our lives. One decision will not make you or break your life. It is the compound effect of all our decisions that determine our results. Life is simple addition: one decision added to another added to another added to another added to another. Each decision, when added together, determines who we are and accounts for where we are in our lives, so don't be afraid to take a shot.

In my school assemblies, I frequently give people opportunities to take a shot to win one of my basketballs. During one evening program with students and their parents, I picked a dad to shoot a shot to win the ball. I gave him two options: Shoot from the three-point line and make it and win the ball; if you miss, you get a Jim "Basketball" Jones pencil. Then his second option was to shoot from the foul line. If he made it, he could also win the ball, but if he missed, he would have to do 10 pushups. The dad picked the three-point shot because doing pushups wasn't his strong point. I then asked if someone in the audience would be willing to help him, and another dad to come out to help him. I asked the second dad, "Would you be willing to do the pushups for him if he missed the closer shot?" "Sure," the guy said. I moved the dad up to the foul line to shoot. I watched what was the ugliest-looking shot I have ever seen fly through the air and hit nothing but net. He won. He looked at me and said, "I have never made a basket in my life. I am the most uncoordinated person on the planet. Today is the best day of my life!" After the show, he bought two more basketballs from me and said,

"These two are for my kids. No one will be allowed to play with the ball I won. I made the shot!" I said, "You made it because you were willing to take a shot!"

After everyone cleared the gym, I laid down on the foul line and just took a breath to take in what happened that night for that dad. He made a shot for the first time in his life because he raised his hand and took a risk to even take the shot. What is holding you back from taking a shot at success? Just take a shot, my friend. You can do it.

 What is your action plan? Write your thoughts down here. Remember, thoughts become actions, and actions bring results.

Write Something! Do Something!

_____

_____

_____

_____

_____

_____

_____

_____

_____

_____

_____

_____

_____

_____

_____

_____

_____

_____

_____

_____

_____

Chapter 9 – Build Your Library

"The more that you read, the more things you will know. The more that you learn, the more placed you'll go."

– Dr. Seuss

The central requirement of life is learning. Success, like everything else, is learned. And success involves a commitment to learning.

Some people are chasing success but would find the chase much easier if they spent more time improving themselves. Keep reading books, listening to audio programs or TED talks, attending seminars, and taking college courses. Because I drive so much to get to my presentations, I have made my car my library, where I listen to books on Audible. Zig Ziglar would suggest to his audiences to listen to books in their cars; he called it enrolling in "Automobile University." I have found listening to the same book or audio program a second or third time always yields new ideas and information. The same helpful message provides fresh insights because of new life circumstances or just because I missed a golden nugget the first time.

I was a lucky child growing up. My dad owned his own company, and because of this, he had us listen to the same motivational material he shared with his sales staff. I was raised on Vince Lombardi and Earl Nightingale, and I was taught the "Greatest Secret" as a boy. It was good stuff, and those lectures had a formative effect on my childhood. Where would I be if not for my dad's library?

When I listen to a new audio program or read a book, most of what I encounter is something that I've heard before. In that sense, new material serves as a wonderful reminder and reinforcement of the best from reading lists past. But it's not just that. I almost always find at least one great new insight from my latest library addition.

One of my favorite authors is Malcolm Gladwell. I have found great life lessons in his books, *Outliers, Tipping Point, David and Goliath*, and *Blink*. Because I work in the education field, I have invested in books like *Mindset* by Carol Dweck, *GRIT* by Angela Duckworth, *Culturize* by Jimmy Casas, *Unselfie* by Michele Borba, *Above the Line* by Urban Meyer, and *The Seven Habits of Highly Effective People* by Stephan Covey, to name just a few.

I can easily listen to 20 hours of books per week. Over the course of a year, investing my driving time in listening to books is significant. Build your library so you can continue to improve and stretch yourself.

What is your action plan? Write your thoughts down here. Remember, thoughts become actions, and actions bring results.

Write Something! Do Something!

_____

_____

_____

_____

_____

_____

_____

_____

_____

_____

_____

_____

_____

_____

_____

_____

_____

_____

_____

_____

Chapter 10 – UBU: You Be You

"To be yourself in a world that is constantly trying to make you something else is the greatest accomplishment."

– Ralph Waldo Emerson

So many people try to influence us to be something because it makes more money, has more prestige, or whatever. The key in everything we are talking about here is being you. Find your passion in life, and do what you love to do. That's the best gift you can give yourself. Don't be afraid to go for it and try to become what you want to be. The key to having a happy life is to pursue something you feel has meaning and purpose. It's easy to get up in the morning when you know what you do will make a difference in one way or another. Sometimes when talking with someone before my show, I will tell them that I am retired. They look at me funny and say, "Your retired?" I repeat it: "I am retired." You see, in retirement, you get to do what you want to do. Being Jim "Basketball" Jones and inspiring people to overcome challenges and keep believing in themselves is exactly what I want to do. So I guess by that definition, I am retired. I hope you find something you can do that doesn't feel like work.

Too many people see what other people have and wish they had their life. Facebook is great at making us feel like we have a boring life compared to everyone else since most people only post good stuff about their life on Facebook. Don't compare yourself to them. You be you, and go after your dreams and goals. Whatever that is for you, it's okay. You are allowed to be unique, creative, happy, fun, and different. Be yourself! You are good enough, worthy enough, and capable enough to become what you want to become. Now go get it done, my friend.

What is your action plan? Write your thoughts down here. Remember, thoughts become actions, and actions bring results.

Write Something! Do Something!

Chapter 11 – Make a Difference

"I might not be able to change the world, but today I can change someone's world."

– Jim "Basketball" Jones

I was visiting an elementary school in the Pittsburgh area and had the audience repeat after me, "I am important, I matter, I'm unique, I'm creative, I work hard, and I was born NOT to be PERFECT but to make a DIFFERENCE." The following year, I was invited back to that school, and a mom was waiting to speak with me before my assembly. She smiled at me and said, "Hey, Basketball Jones, my daughter Kailee quotes you." She went on to explain her daughter has cerebral palsy, and ever since the year before, her little third grade girl had been saying what I had said during my assembly. "When I take her to physical therapy and watch her struggle, I start to cry, and when

Kailee notices, she says, 'Mom, you remember what Basketball Jones said? I'm not born to be perfect, Mom. I'm just born to make a difference. Mom, I'll make a difference.'"

We all have the power to make a difference every day. It doesn't have to be something big or significant. It can be as simple as a "hello." It can be listening to someone, smiling at them, encouraging them, supporting them, or complimenting them.

Growing up in special education really made me feel for kids getting picked on, left out, or bullied. My son Parker had to hear me tell him countless times that he needed to protect and help other kids. I would tell him, "It's not acceptable for kids to be picked on. You are a big kid, and you have to look out for other kids." I think my past was coming out on my son. He handled it well, and I truly think he tried his best to make a difference in school for other kids.

One day when I was picking him up from elementary school, a teacher stopped me and said, "Hey, Basketball Jones, you know what your son has been doing? At lunch time, he asked me if he could sit with my kids. I'm one of the teachers in the new special needs class, and we have been eating at a table by ourselves until that Parker guy came over to be with us. He made friends with one of my nonverbal autistic boys, Michael, and I have seen them together at recess."

Parker told me he had been protecting Michael and hanging around him at recess. Michael liked to throw a ball, and Parker would go get it for him. After a year of hanging out with Michael, Parker said Michael had started to talk, and one of the few words he would say was "Parker."

We all have the ability to spread kindness. All we have to do is DO SOMETHING, and kindness will spread. Like Ellen DeGeneres suggests, buy the person behind you their coffee at Starbucks. These little and simple acts make the world a better place. I feel we should have an intentional purpose to be kind every day. We might not know what and whom our kindness will affect, but we can have an intentional purpose to be kind daily.

Remember, while you are striving to reach your goals, make sure you are making a difference for others. You might not be able to change the world, but today you can change someone's world.

 **What is your action plan? Write your thoughts down here. Remember, thoughts become actions, and actions bring results.**

Write Something! Do Something!

_____

_____

_____

_____

_____

_____

_____

_____

_____

_____

_____

_____

_____

_____

_____

_____

_____

_____

_____

_____

_____

Chapter 12 – Conclusion

"You, are the best YOU ever born. You are UNIQUE, you are IMPORTANT, and you were born to be great!"

– Jim "Basketball" Jones

We all have adversity and challenges as we go through life. It's not bad luck, just life. The power to change, grow, and persevere will determine the life you will live. Remember, a productive and happy life will involve some level of pain and discomfort. You have the ability and power to push through these challenges. Don't settle. Don't be a victim of your circumstances, but be a victor over your challenges. You were born to be great and make a difference in this world, but that means you have to take action and dooooo something. Don't sit back and wait for opportunities to find you. Go make your opportunities. As Les Brown says, "It's much worse to have an opportunity that you are not prepared for than to prepare for an opportunity that never comes." You have to prepare yourself, improve yourself, and challenge yourself, and when you get knocked down, get yourself back up. We all get knocked down, we mess up, and we fail. These are just stepping stones to our success. I hope this book strengthens you to deal with and overcome your life's challenges. I believe in you, and I know you can do it.

I believe your life has purpose and meaning. This world is a better place because you are part of it. Believe, dream, and take a shot. If you miss, who cares? Keep shooting. It's your life, and it's your time to go write your story. You can do it! Here's to YOU!

I wish you all the best,

Jim "Basketball" Jones

Made in the USA
Middletown, DE
06 July 2020

DEC 1 4 2021